GREATEST QUOTATIONS

Edited by :

P.V. GOPALKRISHNAN

Books For All

DELHI

Sales Office:
D.K. Publishers Distributors (P) Ltd.
1.Ansari Road, Darya Ganj.
New Delhi-110002
Phone: 3261465, 3278368
Fax: 091-011-3264368

Published by:
Books For All
B-2, Vardhman Palace,
Nimri Commercial Centre
Near Bharat Nagar, Ashok Vihar
Delhi-110052
Phone: 7401672
Fax: 091-011-7138265

Laser Typeset by:
Print Consultants, Delhi-110001
Phone: 3365334, 3365335
Fax: 3365334

Printed At:
D.K. Fine Art Press (P) Ltd., Delhi-110052

EDITOR'S NOTE

You are living in a complex world. The troubles and tribulation are numerous today. when met with a new problem which is totally alien, You will be perplexed. You cannot decide you cannot understand either, your parents or friends are helpless because of the lack of knowledge or the lack of time but you need a help from a reliable source. This book, is the best source. Almost all of the matters that touch a man's life are arrayed in this book. Great care has been given in selecting not only the subjects but the best among the sayings what makes special this book apart from the other ones in this cottager are its selected subjects and the equal importance to every one of the tables. with the possession of this book you are no longer a pray of Jack of all trades who chats matters from cosmology to cosmetology, you can keep this book as a reference book and glance through it when you need advice.

P.V. Gopalkrishnan

CONTENTS

ANGER

- ☐ Envy and wrath shorten the life.

  ....*Bible*

- ☐ I was angry with my friend;
  I told my warth, my wrath did end.
  I was angry with my foe;
  I told it not, my wrath did grow.

  ....*William Blake*

- ☐ Anger is a brief madness.

  ....*Horace*

- ☐ Anger supplies the arms.

  ....*Virgil*

- ☐ Anger is like
  A full-hot horse, who being allowed his way, self-mettle tries him.

  ....*Shakespeare*

- ☐ The tigers of wrath are wiser than the horses of instruction.

  ....*William Blake*

- ☐ Anger makes dull men witty, but it keeps them poor.

  ....*Elizabeth-I*

- ☐ When angry, count four, When very angry, swear.

  ....*Mark Twain*

BEAUTY

- ☐ Remember that the most beautiful things in the world are most useless, peacocks and lilies, for example.

  ....*John Ruskin*

- ☐ There is no excellent beauty that hath not some strangeness in the proportion.

  ....*Francis Bacon.*

- ☐ Beauty is a short-lived reign.

  ....*Socrates*

- ☐ What is beautiful is good and who is good will soon also be beautiful.

  ....*Sappho*

- ☐ Beauty is in the eye of the beholder.

  ....*Margaret Hungerford*

- ☐ Beauty is truth, truth beauty-that is all ye know on earth, and all ye need to know.

  ....*John Keats*

- ☐ It is amazing how complete is the delusion that beauty is goodness.

  ....*Leo Tolstoy.*

- ☐ What is lovely never dies, But passes into other loveliness.

  ....*Thomas Bailey Aldrich*

BLISS

- ☐ It was a dream of perfect bliss,Too beautiful to last.

  ........*T.N. Bayly*

- ☐ Scenes where love and bliss immortal reign.

  ....*Thomson*

- ☐ Rejoice and men will seek you
  Grieve, and they turn and go;
  They want full measure of all your pleasure,
  But they do not need your woe.

  ....*Ella Wheeler wilcoz*

- ☐ I have drunken deep of joy,
  And I will taste no other wine to-night.

  ....*Shelley*

- ☐ But we are pressed by heavy laws; And often, glad no more,
  we wear a face of joy, because, we have been glad of yore.

  ....*Wordsworth.*

- ☐ All human Joys are Swift of wing, For heaven doth so allot it,
  That when you get an easy thing,You find you haven't got it.

  ....*Engene Field.*

- ☐ Joy comes, grief goes, we know not how.

  ........*J.R. Lowell.*

BOLDNESS

- ☐ And dar'st thou then, To beard the lion in his den,
The Douglas in his hall?

.........Scott.

- ☐ The die is Cast.

.........Julius Caesar

- ☐ He who seizes the right moment, Is the right man.

.........Goethe

- ☐ Fortune sides with him who dares.

..................Virgil

- ☐ I dare do all that may become a man, who dares do more is none.

.........Shakespeare

- ☐ He either fears his fate too much,
Or his deserts are small,
That dares not put it to the touch,
To gain or lose it all.

.........James Graham

- ☐ There is a tide in the affairs of men
which, taken at the flood,leads on to fortune,
Omitted, all the voyage of their life
Is bound in shallows and in miseries.

.........Shakespeare

Book

- ☐ Some books are to be tasted, others to be swallowed, and some few to be chewed and digested.....

  ....*Bacon*

- ☐ Camerado, this is no book, Who touches this, touches a man.......

  ....*Walt Whitman*

- ☐ I trust in God- and in good books.

  ....*Campbell*

- ☐ A good book is the best of friends, the same today and forever.

  ....*Martin F. Tupper*

- ☐ Books are the treasured wealth of the world and the fit inheritance of generations and nations.

  ....*Thorean*

- ☐ We should n't teach great books, we should teach a love of reading.

  ........*B.F. Skinner*

- ☐ How many a man has dated a new era in his life from the reading of a book.

  ....*Ibid*

- ☐ I cannot live without books.

  ....*Thomas Jefferson*

CARE

- ☐ And the night shall be filled with music, And the cares, that infest the day, Shall fold their tents, like the Arabs, And as Silently steal away.

  ....*Longfellow*

- ☐ Ye banks and braes O'bonnie Doon, How can ye bloom sae fresh and fair? How can ye Chant, ye little birds, and I sae weary fu'o'care?

  ....*Burns*

- ☐ To carry care to bed, is to sleep with a pack on your back.

  ....*Haliburton*

- ☐ Care kills a cat
  To carry to bed is to sleep with a pack on your back,
  The wife of a careless man is always a widow.

  ....*Hungarian Proverbs*

- ☐ Be slow of tongue and quick of eye when buying use your eyes rather than your ears. The cautions seldom err.

  ....*Chinese Proverbs*

- ☐ Drink nothing without seeing, sing nothing without reading it.

  ....*Spanish Proverb.*

CHARACTER

- No Character moves up or down, At other's smile or others frown;
  But honour or contempt on earth, Will follow conduct's inner worth.

  ....*Panchatantra*

- Character is what you are in the dark.

  ....*Dwight L. Moody*

- Don't say things. What you are stands over you the while, and thunders so that I cannot hear what you say to the contrary.

  ....*Emerson*

- Fame is what you have taken, Character's what you give,
  When to this truth you waken, Then you begin to live.

  ....*Bayard Taylor*

- Good name in man and woman, dear my lord,
  Is the immediate jewel of their souls: Who steals my purse steals trash........
  But he that filches from me my good name
  Robs me of that which not enriches him, And makes me poor indeed.

  ....*Shakespeare*

- When wealth is lost, nothing is lost;
  When health is lost, something is lost;
  When character is lost, everything is lost.

  ....*Smiles*

CIVILIZATION

- ☐ Civilization is a progress from an indefinite, incoherent homogeneity towards a definite, coherent, heterogeneity.

  ....*Herbert Spencer*

- ☐ Civilization means a society based upon the opinion of Civilians. It means that violence, the rule of warriors and despotic chiefs, the conditions of campus and warfare, of riot and tyranny, give place to parliaments where laws are made, and independent courts of justice in which over long periods those laws are maintained.

  ....*Winston Churchill*

- ☐ Civilization is the progress towards a society of privacy.

  ....*Ayn Rand*

- ☐ What men call Civilization, always results in deserts.

  ....*Don Marquis*

- ☐ Civilization advances by extending the number of important operations which we can perform without thinking about them.

  ....*Alfred North*

- ☐ You can't say civilization don't advance.....
  in every war they kill you in a new way.

  ....*Will Rogers*

CLOTHES

- Beware of all enterprises that require new clothes.

........*Thorean*

- The sense of being well-dressed gives a feeling of inward tranquillity which religion is powerless to bestow.

........*Emerson*

- Good clothes open all doors.

........*Thomas Fuller*

- All dressed up, with nowhere to go.

........*William Allen White*

- A sweet disorder in the dress, Kindles in clothes a wantonness.

........*Herrick*

- Still to be neat, still to be drest, As you were going to a feast,
  Still to be powder'd, still perfumed.

........*Ben Johnson*

- The tulip and the butterfly, Appear in gayer coats than I,
  Let me be dressed fine as I will, Flies, worms, and flowers exceeds me still.

........*Isaac Watts*

COMPANION

- Associate yourself with men of good quality if you esteem your own reputation; for 'tis better to be alone than in bad company.

  ....*George Washington*

- A man is known by the company he keeps Two's company, three's crowd.

  ....*Hindustani Proverb*

- I have had playmates, I have had companions,
  In my days of Childhood, in my joyful school days,
  All, all are gone, the old familiar faces.

  ....*Charles Lamb*

- A friend in need is a friend indeed. Prosperity makes friends but adversity tries them A friend is one who dislikes the same people you dislike. A true friends is one soul in two bodies. The only way to have a friend is to be a friend. Reprove your friend in secret, praise him openly, True friendship is a plant of slow growth. A back friend, a shoulder clapper.

  ....*Shakespeare*

- Elysium is as far as to ,The very nearest room,
  If in that room a friend await,Felicity or doom.

  ....*Emily Dickinson*

COMPROMISE

- ☐ From compromise and things half done, keep me with stern and stubborn pride, And when at last the fight is won,God, keep me still unsatisfied.

  ....*Louis Untermeyer*

- ☐ They enslave children's children who make compromise with sin.

  ....*Lowell*

- ☐ Better bend than break.

  ....*Scottish Proverb*

- ☐ Some men are born mediocre, some men achieve mediocrity, and some men have mediocrity thrust upon them with major, major it had been all three.

  ....*Joseph Hellor*

- ☐ The only sin is mediocrity.

  ....*Martha Graham*

- ☐ The world is a republic of mediocrities, and always was.

  ....*Thomas Carlyle*

- ☐ There are certain things in which mediocrity is insupportable-poetry, music, painig, public speaking.

  ....*La Bruyere*

CONFESS

- To confess a fault freely is the next thing to being innocent of it.

  ....*Syrus*

- Confess yourself to heaven,
  Repent what's past, avoid what is to come,
  And do not spread the compost on the weeds, To make them ranker.

  ....*Shakespeare*

- One who tells all he knows will also tell what he does not.
  God forgives those who sincerely confess.

  ....*Scottish Proverb*

- Confession of error is like a broom that sweeps away dirt and leaves the surface cleaner than before.

  ....*Mahatma Gandhi*

- The best composition and temperature is to have openness in fame and opinion, Secrecy in habit, dissimulation in seasonable use, and a power to feign, if there be no remedy.

  ....*Bacon*

- Openness is the best policy.

  ....*A. Proverb*

CONFIDENCE

- ☐ They can do all because they think they can.

  ....*Virgil*

- ☐ Who has self-confidence will lead the rest.

  ....*Horace*

- ☐ Be always sure you're right, then go ahead.

  ....*Davy Crockett*

- ☐ By mutual confidence and mutual aid great deeds are done, and great discoveries made.

  ....*Homer*

- ☐ Know then thyself, presume not God to scan,
  The proper study of mankind is man.

  ....*Pope*

- ☐ Confidence carries conviction, Society is built upon trust,Blind belief is better than no belief, Skill and confidence are an unconquered army.

  ....*American Proverb*

- ☐ The bullet that will kill me is not yet cast.

  ....*Napoleon Bonaparte*

- ☐ I bear a charmed life.

  ....*Shakespeare*

- ☐ Ask, and it shall be given you; seek, and ye shall find; knock, and it shall be opened unto you.

  ....*Bible*

CONSCIENCE

- ☐ Conscience is God's presence in man.

  ....*Swedenberg*

- ☐ Trust that man is nothing who has not a conscience in everything.

  ....*Sterne*

- ☐ Conscience is the inner voice that warns us some body may be looking.

  .........*H.L. Mencken*

- ☐ I cannot and will not cut my conscience to suit this year's fashions.

  ....*Lillian Hellman*

- ☐ This conscience does make cowards of us all; and thus the native hue of resolution, Is sicklied o'er with the pale cast of thought.

  ....*Shakespeare*

- ☐ There is no pillow so soft as a clean conscience.

  ....*French Proverb*

- ☐ Conscience is the perfect interpreter of life.

  ....*Karl Barth*

- ☐ That fierce thing, They call a conscience !

  ....*Hood*

COURAGE

- ☐ The greatest test of courage on earth is to bear defeat without losing heart.

  ........*R.G. Ingersoll*

- ☐ Cowards die many times before their deaths;
  The Valiant never taste of death but once.

  ....*Shakespeare*

- ☐ Courage is resistance to fear, mastery of fear-not absence of fear.

  ....*Mark Twain*

- ☐ Often the test of courage is not to die but to live.

  ....*Vittorio Alfieri*

- ☐ Tender-handed stroke a nettle, And it stings you for your pains,
  Grasp it like a man of mettle, And it soft as silk remains.

  ....*Aaron Hill*

- ☐ Until the day of his death, no man can be sure of his courage.

  ....*Jean Anouilh*

- ☐ What though the field be lost? All is not lost, the' unconquerable will,
  And study of revenge, immortal hate, And courage never to submit or yield.

  ....*Milton*

CRIME

- ☐ Murder will be out.
  One crime is everything, two nothing. As well be hanged for a cow as for a hen. It is not the thief who is hanged, but one who is caught stealing.
  ....*A Proverb*

- ☐ Many a crime deemed innocent on earth is registered in heaven.
  ....*Cowper*

- ☐ It's a wicked world, and when a clever man turns his brains to crime, it is the worst of all.
  ....*Conan Doyle*

- ☐ And who are the greater criminals-those who sell the instruments of death, or those who buy them and use them.
  ....*Robert E. Sherwood.*

- ☐ These, having not the law, are a law unto themselves.
  ....*Bible*

- ☐ The soul of a murder is blind.
  ....*Albert Camus*

- ☐ Successful crimes alone are Justified.
  ....*Dryden*

CRISES

- ☐ It was the best of times, it was the worst of times, it was the age of wisdom, it was the age of foolishness, it was the epoch of belief, it was the epoch of incredulity, it was the season of Light, it was the season of Darkness, it was the spring of hope, it was the winter of despair, we had everything before us, we had nothing before us, we were all going direct to Heaven, we were all going direct the other way.

  ....*Charles Dickens*

- ☐ These are the times that try men's souls.

  ....*Thomas Paine*

- ☐ Chaos often breeds life, when order breeds habit.

  ....*Henry Brooks Adams*

- ☐ The time is out of Joint; O Cursed spite, That ever I was born to set it right.

  ....*Shakespeare*

- ☐ Into each life some rain must fall, some days must be dark and dreary.

  ....*Henry Wadsworth Longfellow*

- ☐ A wonded deer-leaps highest.

  ....*Emily Dickinson*

CRUELTY

- ☐ Of all beasts the man beast is the worst, To others and himself the cruellest foe.

  ....*R. Boxter*

- ☐ With malice toward none, with charity for all, with firmness in the right, as God gives us to see the right.

  ....*Lincoln*

- ☐ The despot, be assured, lives night and day like one condemned to death by the whole of mankind for his wickedness.

  ....*Xenophon*

- ☐ When a nation has allowed itself to fall under a tyrannical regime, it cannot be absolved from the faults due to the guilt of that regime.

  ....*Winston Churchill*

- ☐ Why, man, he doth bestride the narrow world like a colossus.

  ....*Shakespeare*

- ☐ Big Brother is watching you.

  ....*George Orwell*

- ☐ I must be cruel, only to be kind.

  ....*Shakespeare*

DEATH

- ☐ Because I could not stop for death; He kindly stopped for me-
  The carriage held but just ourselves, And Immortality.

  ....Emily Dickinson

- ☐ It hath often been said that it is not death but dying that is terrible.

  ....Henry Fielding

- ☐ Dying is an art, like everything else.

  ....*Sylvia Plath*

- ☐ Whom the gods love die young.

  ....*Menander*

- ☐ There is no death, only a change of worlds.

  ....*Seattle*

- ☐ Death is not an event in life, we do not experience death.

  ....*Ludwig Wittgenstein*

- ☐ We fear death as children fear to go into the dark.

  ....*Bacon*

- ☐ O Death! the poor man's, dearest friend-The kindest and the best.

  ....*Burns*

DECEIVE

- ☐ O, what a tangled web we weave,
  when first we practice to deceive!

  ....*Walter Scott*
- ☐ You can fool some of the people all of the time, and all of the people some of the time, but you cannot fool all of the people all the time.

  ....*Lincoln*
- ☐ Unless a man feels he has a good enough memory,
  he should never venture to lie.

  ....*Montaigue*
- ☐ Dont lie if you don't have to.

  ....*Leo Szilard*
- ☐ To make a living, craftiness is better than learnedness.

  ........*P.A.C. De Beaumarchais*
- ☐ The fox knows many tricks, but the hedgehog's trick is the best of all.

  ....*Pigres*
- ☐ Make to yourselves friends of the mammon of unrighteousness.

  ....*Bible*
- ☐ I know a trick worth two of that.

  ....*Shakespeare*

DESIRE

- There are two tragedies in life, one is not to get your heart's desire.
  The other is to get it.

........Bernard Shaw

- The desire of the moth for the star, Of the night for the morrow,
  The devotion to something afar, From the sphere of our sorrow.

........Shelley

- If wishes were horses, beggards would ride
  The wish is father to the thought.
  If men can halve their wishes, they can double their achievements.

........A. Proverb

- From the desert I came to thee
  On a stallion shod with fire;
  And the winds are left behind
  In the speed of my desire.

........Bayard Taylor

- I wish I hadn't broke that dish,
  I wish I was a movie-star,
  I wish a lot of things, I wish
  That life was like the movies are.

........A.P. Herbert

DESTINY

☐ If God in His wisdom have brought close the day when I must die,That day by water or fire or air my feet shall fall in the destined share wherever my road may lie.

........D.G. Rossetti

☐ Hanging and wiving go by destiny.

........Shakespeare

☐ Destiny never swerves, Nor yields to man the helm,
He shoots his thought, by hidden nerves, Throughout the solid realm.

........Emerson

☐ I want to seize fate by the throat.

........Ludwig Van Beethoven

☐ A man's character is his fate.

........Heraclitus

☐ I claim not to have controlled events, but confess plainly that events have controlled me.

........Abraham Lincoln

☐ For man is man and master of his fate.

........Alfred, Lord Tennyson.

☐ Every man meets his Waterloo at last.

........Hindi Proverb

DISOBEDIENCE

- Of man's first disobedience, and the fruit of that forbidden tree, whose mortal taste, Brought death into the world, and all our woe.

  ....*Milton*

- Obedience
  Bane of all genius, virtue, freedom, truth, makes slaves of men, and, of the human frame, A mechanized automaton.

  ........*P.B. Shelly*

- Rebellion to tyrants is obedience to God.

  ....*Anon*

- Now these are the laws of the Jungle, and many and mighty are they,
  But the head and the hoof of the law and the haunch and the hump is-obey!

  ....*Kipling*

- Where obstinay takes his sturdy stand, To disconcert what policy has planned.

  ....*Cowper*

- The eye that mocketh at his father, and despiseth to obey his mother, the ravens of the valley shall pack it out, and the young eagles shall eat it.

  ....Bible

DOUBT

- Life is doubt, and faith without doubt is nothing but death.

  ....*Miguel De Vnamuno*

- Great intellects are skeptical.

  ....*Friedrich Nietzsche*

- The pragmatist knows that doubt is an art which has to be acquired with difficulty.

  ........*C.S. Peirce*

- If you would be a real seeker after truth, you must at least once in your life doubt, as far as possible, all things.

  ....*Descartes*

- There lives more faith in honest doubt, Believe me, than in half the creeds.

  ....*Tennyson*

- Doubt thou the stars are fire, Doubt that the sun doth move,
  Doubt truth to be a liar, But never doubt I love.

  ....*Shakespeare*

- Our doubts are traitors, Doubt destroys deeds
  Who knows most, doubts not,when in doubt, win the trick.

  ....*Edmuned Hoyle*

DRESS

- The tulip and the butterfly, Appear in grayer coats than I :
  Let me be dressed fine as I will, Flies, worms, and flowers exceed me still.

  ....*Isaac Watts*

- Still to be neat, still to be drest,
  As you were going to a feast,
  Still to be powder'd, still perfumed.

  ....*Ben Johnson*

- Costly thy habit as thy purse can buy, But not expressed in fancy, rich not gaudy, for the apparel oft proclaims the man.

  ....*Shakespeare*

- Eat to please yourself but dress to please others. Tailor makes a man, clothes make a man, It is only fine feathers that make fine birds.

  ....*A Hindi Proverb*

- A sweet disorder in the dress, Kindles in clothes a wantonness.

  ....*Herrick*

- Where's the man could ease a heart like a satin gown?

  ....*Dorothy Parker*

DRINK

- ☐ The more you drink the more you crave.

  ....*Horace*

- ☐ Drink to me only with thine eyes, and I will pledge with thine,
  Or leave a kiss but in the cup, and I'll not look for wine.

  ....*Ben Johnson*

- ☐ O God, that men should put an enemy in their mouths to steal away their brains! That we should, with joy, pleasance, revel and applause, transform ourselves into beasts.

  ....*Shakespeare*

- ☐ Though in silence, with blighted affection, I pine, yet the lips that touch liquor must never touch mine!

  ....*George W. Young*

- ☐ Better sleep with a sober cannibal than a drunken christian.

  ....*Herman Melville*

- ☐ Candy, Is dandy, But liquor, Is quicker.

  ....*Ogden Nash*

- ☐ It's a long time between drinks.

  ....*Stevenson*

DUTY

- ☐ I slept and dreamed that life was beauty, I woke, and found that life was duty.
  ....*Ellen S. Hooper*
- ☐ Do thy duty which lies nearest thee, which thou knowest to be a duty! The second duty will already become clearer.
  ....*T. Carlyle*
- ☐ The dutiful are beautiful. England expects everyone to do his duty.
  ....*Lord Nelson*
- ☐ Do noble things, do not dream them all day long.
  ....*Charles Kingsley*
- ☐ Men are all alike in their promises. It is only in their deeds that they differ.
  ....*Moliere*
- ☐ No one knows what he can do till he tries.
  ....*Publilius Syrus*
- ☐ Our nature lies in movements, complete rest is death.
  ....*Pascal*
- ☐ Our deeds determine us, as much as we determine our deeds.
  ....*George Eliot*

EDUCATION

- What's a' your jargon of your schools, your Latin names for horns and stools, If honest Nature made you fools.

  ....*Burns*

- Each one, teach one, Each alive, teach five
  Let us mend our education or end our education
  Mal-education is worse than noon-education. True education is not a purchasable commodity, It cannot be brought and sold. Learn to teach; teach to learn
  Learn to live before you live to learn, Live and learn
  Learn by earning; earn by learning, There is no education like adversity.

  ....*Proverb*

- A little learning is a dangerous thing.

  ....*Alexander Pope*

- Knowledge itself is power.

  ....*Francis Bacon*

- Education is freedom.

  ....*Andr Gide*

- The direction in which education starts a man will determine his future life.

  ....*Plato*

ENEMY

- ☐ It is impossible for any man not to have some enemies.

  ....*Lord Chesterfield*

- ☐ I choose my friends for their good looks, my acquaintances for their good characters, and my enemies for their good intellects. A man cannot be too careful in the choice of his enemies.

  ....*Oscar wilde*

- ☐ He makes no friend who never make a foe.

  ....*Alfred, Lord Tennyson*

- ☐ The art of leadership...... consists in consolidating the attention of the people against a single adversary and taking care that nothing will split up that attention.

  ....*Adolf Hitler.*

- ☐ You shall judge of a man by his foes as well as by friends.

  ....*Joseph Conrad*

- ☐ We have met the enemy and they are ours.

  ....*Oliver Hazard Perry*

- ☐ If thine enemy hunger, feed him, If he thirst, give him drink, for in so doing thou shalt heap coals of fire on his head.

  ....*New Testament*

ENVY

- ☐ The most anti-social and obvious of all passions, envy.

  .........*J.S. Mill*

- ☐ Base envy withers at another's joy,
  And hates that excellence it cannot reach.

  ....*Thomson*

- ☐ I can endure my own despair,
  But not another's hope.

  ....*William Walsh*

- ☐ O, beware, my lord of Jealousy, It is the green-eyed monster which doth mock, The meat it feeds on.

  ....*Shakespeare*

- ☐ Jealousy it always born with love, but does not always die with it.

  ....*La Rochefoucauld.*

- ☐ There is no greater glory than love, nor any greater punishment than jealousy.

  ....*Lope De Vega*

- ☐ Love is as strong as death, Jealousy is as cruel as the grave.

  ....*Bible*

ERROR

- All men are liable to error, and most men are, in many points, by passion or interest, under temptation to it.

  ....*John Locke*

- Thou art weighed in the balances, and are found wanting.

  ....*Bible*

- Error is the force that welds men together, truth is communicated to men only by deeds of truth.

  ....*Tolstoy*

- Errors like straws, upon the surface flow,
  He who would search for pearls must dive below.

  ....*Dryden*

- To err is human, to forgive divine the catious seldom err.

  ....*Chineese Proverb*

- Truth, crushed to earth, shall rise again, the eternal years of God are hers, But error, wounded, writhes in pain, and dies among his worshippers.

  ....*William C. Bryant.*

- Mistakes live in the neighborhood of truth and therefore delude us.

  ....*Rabindranath Tagore*

EVIL

- ☐ Evil by itself has no legs to stand upon.

  ........*M.K. Gandhi*
- ☐ Of two evils the less is always to be chosen.

  ....*Thomas Kempis*
- ☐ All human evil comes from this, a man's being unable to sit still in a room.

  ....*Theodore Roosevelt*
- ☐ Wickedness is always easier than virtue, for it takes the short cut to everything.

  ....*Samuel Johnson*
- ☐ A man does not sin by commission only, but often by comission.

  ....*Marcus Aurelius*
- ☐ He who accepts evil without protesting against it is really co-operating with it.

  ....*Martin Luther King*
- ☐ Evil it wrought by want of Thought as well as want of Heart.

  ....*Thomas Hood.*
- ☐ For every evil under the sun,
There is a remedy, or there is none,
If there be one, try and find it,
If there be none, never mind it.

  ........*W.C. Hazlitt*

FALSE

- ☐ False in one thing, false in everything.

  ....*Proverb*

- ☐ All was false and hollow, though his tongue dropped manna, and could make the worse appear the better reason.

  ....*Milton*

- ☐ One false step is never retrieved.

  ....*Gray*

- ☐ O what a goodly outside falsehood hath.

  ....*Shakespeare*

- ☐ The wrong always seems the more reasonable.

  ....*George Moore*

- ☐ A lie is an abomination unto the Lord and a very present help in trouble.

  .... *Adlai Stevenson*

- ☐ Let not thy left hand know what thy right hand doeth.

  ....*Bible*

- ☐ Once to every man and nation comes the moment to decide.
  In the strife of truth with falsehood, for the good or evil side.

  ....*Lowell*

FRIENDSHIP

- ☐ Friendship's the wine of life, but friendship new is neither strong nor pure.

  ....*Young*

- ☐ Friendship needs no words-it is solitude delivered from the anguish of loneliness.

  ....*Dag Hammarskjold*

- ☐ Have no friends not equal to yourself.

  ....*Confucius*

- ☐ May God defend me from my friends, I can defend myself from my enemies.

  ....*Due De Villars*

- ☐ Love is only chatter, Friends are all that matter.

  ....*Gelett Burgess*

- ☐ Most friendship is feigning, most loving mere folly.

  ....*Shakespeare*

- ☐ When I remember all
  The friends, so linked together, I've seen around me fall,
  Like leaves in wintry weather, I feel like one
  Who treads alone, Some banquet-hall deserted...

  ....*Moore*

FUTURE

- I never think of future. It comes soon enough.

  ....*Einstein*

- Trust no future, however pleasant! Let the dead past bury its dead!

  ....*Longfellow*

- The highest wisdom is never to worry about the future but to resign ourselves entirely to His will.

  ........*M.K. Gandhi*

- When all is lost, future still remains.

  ....*A. Hindi Proverb*

- In the long run...... we are all dead.

  ....*John Maynard Keynes*

- If you want a picture of the future, Imagine a boot stamping on a human face-forever.

  ....*George Orwell*

- Heaven from all creatures hides the Book of fate, All but the page prescribed, their present state, from brutes what men, from men what spirits know, or who could suffer being here below?

  ....*Pope*

- I hold that man is in the right who is most closely in league with the future.

  ....*Henrik Ibsen*

GAMBLING

- ☐ Cards are war in disguise of a sport.

  ....*Charles Lamb*

- ☐ The roulette table pays nobody except him who keeps it. Neverthless, a passion for gaming is common, though a passion for keeping roulette wheels is unknown.

  ....*George Bernard Shaw*

- ☐ It is the child of avarice, the brother of inequality, and the father of mischief.

  ....*George Washington*

- ☐ There are two times in a man's life when he should not speculate, when he can't afford it, and when he can.

  ....*Mark Twain*

- ☐ And once or twice to throw the dice, Is a gentlemanly game,
  But he does not win who plays with sin,In the secret house of shame.

  ....*Oscar Wilde*

- ☐ In my schooldays, when I had lost one shaft, I shot his fellow of the self-same flight the self-same way, with more advised watch, to find the other forth; and by advent'ring both ,I oft found both.

  ....*Shakespeare*

GENEROSITY

- ☐ He gives twice who gives promptly.

  ....*Publilius Surus*

- ☐ He is rich who hath enough to be charitable.

  ....*Sir Thomas Browne*

- ☐ It is more blessed to give than to receive.

  ....*Bible*

- ☐ There was a man, though some did think him mad, the more he cast away, the more he had.

  ....*Bunyan*

- ☐ Let the man who has and doesn't give Break his neck, and cease to live!
  Let him who gives without a care, Gather rubies from the air.

  ....*James Stephens*

- ☐ Behold, I do not give lectures or a little charity, when I give I give myself.

  ....*Walt Whitman*

- ☐ What is there more kindly than the feelings between host and guest?

  ....*Aeschylus*

- ☐ With malice toward none, with charity for all.

  ....*Lincoln*

GENTLENESS

☐ Your gentleness shall force
more than your force to move us to gentleness.

........*Shakespeare*

☐ O grant me, Heaven, a middle state, Neither too humble nor too great, more than enough for nature's ends, with something left to treat my friends.

........*David Mallet*

☐ Never eat at a place called Mom's. Never play cards, with a man named Doc. And never lie down with a woman who's got more troubles than you.

........*Nelson Algren*

☐ Trust everybody, but cut the cards.

........*Finley Peter Dunne*

☐ Be not the first by whom the new are tried, nor yet the last to lay the old aside.

........*Alexander Pope*

☐ Put all your eggs in one basket-and watch that basket.

........*Mark Twain*

☐ If you want to get along, go along.

........*Sam Rayburn*

GLAD

- ☐ Be glad, and your friends are many, be sad, and you lose them all; There are none to decline your nectared wine, But alone you must drink life's gall.

  ....*Ella Wheeler Wilcox*

- ☐ Don't cheer, boys; the poor devils are dying.

  ....*Capt. John W. Philip*

- ☐ Hence, Vain deluding Joys,
  The brood of folly, without father bred.

  ....*Milton*

- ☐ But we are pressed by heavy laws, And often, Glad no more,
  We wear a face of Joy, Because, We have been glad of yore.

  ....*Wordsworth*

- ☐ I found more joy in sorrow, Than you could find in joy.

  ....*Sara Teasdale*

- ☐ Thing won are done, Joy's Soul lies in the doing.

  ....*Shakespeare*

- ☐ Joys too exquisite to last.

  ....*James Mortgomary*

GOD

- ☐ God moves in a mysterious way, His wonders to perform;
  He plants his footsteps in the sea, And rides upon the storm.

  ....*Cowper*

- ☐ God is truth and light his shadow.

  ....*Plato*

- ☐ If God did not exist, it would be necessary to invent him.

  ....*Voltaire*

- ☐ It is better to have no opinion of God at all than such an opinion as is unworthy of Him.

  ....*Bacon*

- ☐ To thee I turn, to thee I make my prayer, God of the open air.

  ....*Henry Van Dyke*

- ☐ God, to me, it seems, is a verb.

  ....*R. Buckminster*

- ☐ My dear child, you must believe in God despite what the clergy tell you.

  ....*Benjamin Jowett*

GOOD

- O' yet we trust that some how good, will be the final goal of ill,
  To pangs of nature, sins of will,Defects of doubt, and taints of blood.

  ....*Tennyson*

- There is no good, there is no bad; these be the whims of mortal will;
  That works me weal that I call "good", what harms and hurts me I hold as "ill".

  ....*Sir Richard Burton*

- If you can keep your head when all about you are losing theirs and blaming it on you,If you can trust yourself when all men doubt you,
  And make allowance for their douting, too.

  ....*Rudyard Kipling*

- Do good by stealth, and blush to find it fame.

  ....*Alexander Pope*

- Virtue may be assailed, but never hurt surprised by unjust force,
  but not enthralled.

  ....*John Milton*

- That best portion of a good man's life, His little, nameless,
  unremembered acts of kindness and of love.

  ....*Wordsworth*

GRIEF

- ☐ I sometimes hold it half a sin, To put in words the grief I feel;
  For words, like nature, half reveal,and half conceal the soul within.

  ....*Tennyson*

- ☐ Grief makes one hour ten.

  ....*-Shakespeare*

- ☐ No blessed leisure for love or hope, But only times for grief.

  ....*Thomas Hood*

- ☐ Into each life some rain must fall,
  Some days must be dark and dreary.

  ....*Longfellow*

- ☐ Heavy the sorrow that bows the head
  When love is alive and hope is dead.

  ........*W.S. Gilbert*

- ☐ Who ne'er his bread in sorrow ate, Who ne'er the mournful midnight hours weeping upon his bed has sate,He knows you not, ye heavenly powers.

  ....*Goethe*

- ☐ Earth has no sorrow that Heaven cannot heal.

  ....*Thomas Moore*

HABIT

- ☐ Habit is the enormous fly-wheel of society, its most precious conservative agent.

  ....*William James*

- ☐ Habit with him was all the test of truth,
  "It must be right; I've done it from my youth".

  ....*George Crabbe*

- ☐ Ill habits gather by unseen degrees,
  As brooks make rivers, rivers run to seas.

  ....*Dryden*

- ☐ Small habits, well persued betimes may reach the dignity of crimes.

  ....*Hannal More*

- ☐ To fall into a habit is to begin to cease to be.

  ....*Mignel De Vnamuno*

- ☐ The nature of men it always the same;
  it is their habits that seperate them.

  ....*Confucius*

- ☐ Habit is a second nature that prevents us from knowing the first, of which it has neither the cruelties nor the enchantments.

  ....*Proust*

- ☐ No this is more powerful than habit.

  ....*Ovid*

HAPPINESS

- ☐ Happiness is an imaginery condition formerly often attributed by the living to the dead, now usually attributed by adults to children, and by children to adults.

  ....*Thomas szasz*

- ☐ All seek joy, but it is not found on earth.

  ....*St. John Chrysostom*

- ☐ The latter end of joy is woe.

  ....*Geoffrey Chancer*

- ☐ A lifetime of happiness! no man alive could bear it; it would be hell on earth.

  ....*Bernard Shaw*

- ☐ The happy only are the truly great.

  ....*Young*

- ☐ Happiness depends on what you can give, not what you can get.

  ........*M.K. Gandhi*

- ☐ Happiness is the only good, reason the only torch, justice the only worship, humanity the only religion, and love the only priest.

  ........*R.G. Ingersoll*

- ☐ That action it best which procures the greatest happiness for the greatest numbers.

  ....*Francis Hutcheson*

HATE

- ☐ Hated by fools, and fools to hate, Be that my motto and my fate.

  ....*Swift*

- ☐ Folks never understand the folk they hate.

  ....*Lowell*

- ☐ Heaven has no rage like love to hatred turned, Nor hell a fury like a woman scorned.

  ....*Willian Congreve*

- ☐ It is human to hate those whom we have injured.

  ....*Tacitus*

- ☐ Now hatred is by far the longest pleasure; Men love in haste, but they detest at leisure.

  ....*Lord Byron*

- ☐ For him who fain would teach the world, The world holds hate in fee—
  For Socrates, the hemlock cup; for christ, gethsemane

  ....*Don Marquis*

- ☐ Violent antipathies are always suspicious, and betray a secret affinity.

  ....*William Hazlitt*

- ☐ Hatred watches while friendship sleeps.

  ....*French Proverb.*

HONESTY

- ☐ An honest man is the noblest work of God.

  ....*Alexander Pope*

- ☐ Being entirely honest with oneself is a good exercise.

  ....*Freud*

- ☐ If you do not tell the truth about yourself you cannot tell it about other people.

  ....*Virginia Woolf.*

- ☐ God looks at the clean hands, not the full ones.

  ....*Publilius Syrus*

- ☐ An honest man's word is as good as his bond.

  ....*Cervantes*

- ☐ Honesty is the best policy.

  ....*Byron*

- ☐ No legacy is so rich as honesty.

  ....*Shakespeare*

- ☐ A prince can mak a belted knight, A marquis, duke, an'a' that,
  But an honest man's aboon his might, Guid faith, he maunna fa' that!

  ....*Burns*

HOPE

- None without hope e'er loved the brightest fair, But love can hope where reason would despair.

  ....*Lord Lyttleton*

- While there is life there's hope.

  ....*Gay*

- True hope is swift, and flies with swallow's wings kings it makes gods, and meaner creature kings.

  ....*Shakespeare*

- Abandon hope, all ye who enter here.

  ....*Dante*

- We did not dare to breath a prayer, or give our anguish scope!
  Something was dead in each of us, And what was dead was Hope.

  ....*Oscar Wilde*

- Still nursing the unconquerable hope,Still clutching the inviolable shade.

  ....*Matthew Arnold*

- Hope, like the gleaming, Taper's light, Adorns and cheers our way;
  And still, as darker grows the night, Emits a lighter ray.

  ....*Oliver Goldsmith.*

HUMILITY

- ☐ Who so ever shall smite thee on thy right cheek, turn to him the other also.

  ....*New Testament*

- ☐ After crosses and losses, men grow humbler and wiser.

  ....*Fraklin*

- ☐ What I beg from God is poverty.

  ....*Gurmukhi*

- ☐ In humility imitate the earth, water runs down, not up
  He that is down need fears no fall
  Pride goes before a fall
  The higher you go, the lower you will fall, Death is the great leveller
  Sun rises and sets every day o-proverbs, Humble thyself in all things.

  ....*Thomas A. Kempis*

- ☐ ..."umble we are, ′ umble we have been, `umble we shall ever be.

  ....*Dickens*

- ☐ Do unto others as though you were the others.

  ....*Anonymous*

HYPOCRISY

- ☐ With one hand he put
A penny in the urn of poverty
And with the other took a shilling out.

........Robert Pollok

- ☐ For neither man nor angel can discern Hypocrisy,
the only evil that walks Invisible, except to God alone.

........John Milton

- ☐ No man is a hypocrite in his pleasures.

........Samuel Johnson

- ☐ With devotion's usage
And pious action we do sugar o er
The devil himself.

........Shakespeare

- ☐ As for conforming outwardly, and living your own life inwardly,
I don't think much of that.

........Thorean

- ☐ They set the sign of the cross over their outer doors, and sacrifice to their gut and their groin in their inner closets.

........Ben Johnson

- ☐ Hypocrisy is the homage which vice pays to virtue.

........La Rochefoucauld

IDLENESS

- ☐ Idle men are dead all their life long.

  ....*Thomas Fuller*

- ☐ I have all my life long been lying (in bed) till noon, yet I tell all young men, and tell them with great sincerity, that nobody who does not rise early will ever do any good.

  ....*Samuel Johnson*

- ☐ For Satan finds some mischief still, for Idle hand to do.

  ....*Isaac Watts*

- ☐ As idle as a painted ship, Up on a painted ocean.

  ....*Coleridge*

- ☐ He lived a life of going-to-do, And died with nothing done.

  ....*J.Albery*

- ☐ Their only labour was to kill times, And labour dire it is, and weary woe.

  ....*Thomson*

- ☐ Were it not better done, as others use to sport with Amaryllis in the shade, or with the tangles of Neaera's hair?

  ....*Milton*

IGNORANCE

- ☐ Where ignorance is bliss, 'Tis folly to be wise.

  ....*Gray*

- ☐ To be ignorant of one's ignorance is the malady of the ignorant.

  ........*A.B. Alcott*

- ☐ Ignorance is degrading only when found in company with riches.

  ....*Schopenhauer*

- ☐ There is no ignorance but darkness

  ....*Shakespeare*

- ☐ Better be unborn than untaught, for ignorance is the root of misfortune.

  ....*Plato*

- ☐ Ignorance is not innocence, but sin

  ....*Browning*

- ☐ I honestly believe it is better few know nothing than few know what alut so.

  ....*John Billings.*

- ☐ The good are better made by ill, As odours crushed are sweeter still.

  ....*S. Rogers*

IMITATION

- ☐ And the man who plants cabbages imitates too.

  ....*Austin Dobron*

- ☐ Imitation is the sincerest of flattery.

  ........*C.C. colton*

- ☐ Imitation is suicide.

  ....*Emerson*

- ☐ There can be no good imitation without intelligence.

  ....*A Hindi Proverb*

- ☐ Human nature is the same all over the world.

  ....*Earl of Chesterfield*

- ☐ Some for renown, on scraps of learning dote,
  and think they grow immortal as they quote.

  ....*Edward Young*

- ☐ Despise not the discoveries of the wise,
  but acquaint thyself with their proverbs.

  ....*Bible*

- ☐ Next to the originator of a good sentence , is the first quote of it.

  ....*Ralph Waldo Emerson*

IMMORTALITY

- Dust thou art, to dust returnest, Was not spoken of the soul.

  ....*Longfellow*

- This life is but the passage of a day,
  This life is but a pang and all is over,
  But in the life to come which fades notaway,
  Every love shall abide and every lover.

  ....*Christina Rossetti*

- Fool! All that is, at all, Lasts ever past recall;
  Earth changes, but thy soul and God stand sure;
  What entered into thee, That was, is, and shall be;
  Times wheel runs back or stops; potter and clay endure.

  ....*R. Browning*

- I swear I think now that everything without exception has an eternal soul!
  The trees have, rooted in the ground! The weeds of the sea have! the animals!

  ....*Walt Whitman*

- Is there beyond the silent night, An endless day?
  Is death a door that leads to light? We cannot say.

  ........*R.G. Incersoll.*

INSPIRATION

- ☐ There is God within us, and we glow when He stirs us.

.........Ovid

- ☐ Gie me ae spark o' Nature's fire, That's a' the learning I desire,
Then tho I trudge thro' dub an mire, At pleugh or cart,
My muse, tho' hamely in attire, May, touch the heart.

.........Burns

- ☐ What is a failure? It's only a spur, To a man who receives it right, And it makes the spirit within him stir to go in once more and fight. If you never have failed, it's an easy guess you never have known a high success.

.........Edmund Vance Cooke

- ☐ Wake! For the sun behind you eastern height, Has chased the session of the stars from night, And, to the field of Heav'n ascending, strikes the sultan's turret with a shaft of light.

.........Edward Fitzgerald

- ☐ Arise, awake; wake up yourself and awaken others.
Achieve the consummation of life before you pass off -
"Arise, awake and stop not still the goal is reached".

.........Swami Vivekanand

JEALOUSY

- I can endure my own despair, But not another's hope.

  ....*William Walsh*

- Trifles light as air, Are to the jealous confirming strong, As proofs of holy writ.

  ....*Shakespeare*

- There is no greater glory than love, nor any greater punishment than Jealousy.

  ....*Lope De Vega*

- It is not love that is blind, but jealousy.

  ....*Lawrence Durrell*

- Jealousy is nothing but the foolish child of pride.

  ....*Pierre Augustin De Beaumarchains*

- O, beware, my lord, of Jealousy;
  It is the green- eyed monster which doth mock the meat it feeds on.

  ....*Shakespeare*

- Jealousy is always born with love, but does not always die with it.

  ....*La Rochefoucauld*

JUSTICE

- ☐ Live and let live is the rule of common Justice.

  ....*Sir. Roger L'Estrange*

- ☐ Fear not, then, thou child infirm,
  Threr's no God dare wrong a worm.

  ....*Emerson*

- ☐ There are times when even justice brings harm with it.

  ....*Sophocles*

- ☐ The laws of changeless justice bind, Oppressor and oppressed;
  And close as sin and suffering joined, We march to fate abreast.

  ....*John Greenleaf Whittier*

- ☐ Injustice anywhere is a threat to justice everywhere.

  ....*Martin Luther King*

- ☐ Let Justice be done, though the heavens fall.

  ....*Lord Mansfield*

- ☐ Thrice is he arm'd that hath his quarrel just and he but naked, though lock'd up in steel, whose conscience with injustice is corrupted.

  ....*Shakespeare*

KINDNESS

- Have you had a kindness shown? pass it on;
  'Twas not given for thee alone, pass it on;
  Let it travel down the years, Let it wipe another's tears;
  Till in Heaven the deed appears, Pass it on.

  ....*Henry Burton*

- Let me be a little kinder, Let me be a little blinder
  To the faults of those around me.

  ....*Edgar A. Guest*

- Kindness effects more than severity.

  ....*Aesop*

- The essence of greatness is the perception that virtue is enough.

  ....*Emerson*

- That best portion of a good man's life, His little, nameless, unremembered acts of kindness and of love.

  ....*Wordsworth.*

- Always do right. This will gratity some people and astonish the rest.

  ....*Mark Twain*

KNOWLEDGE

- ☐ The gift of knowledge is far higher than that of; "food or clothes;" it is even higher than giving life to a man, because the real life of man consists of knowledge.

  ....*Vivekananda*

- ☐ To know that we know what we know, and that we do not know what we do not know, that is true knowledge.

  ....*Thoreau*

- ☐ Knowledge is power.

  ....*Hobes*

- ☐ Knowledge comes, but wisdom lingers.

  ....*Tennyson*

- ☐ I know nothing except the fact of my ignorance.

  ....*Socrates*

- ☐ I have studied now philosophy, And jurisprudence, medicine and even, alas, theology, From end to end with labor keen; And here, poor fool, with all my lore I stand no wiser than before.

  ....*Goethe*

- ☐ All I know is what I read in the papers.

  ....*Will Rogers*

LEADERSHIP

- ☐ To be a leader of men one must turn one's back on men.

  ....*Havelock Ellis*

- ☐ Uneasy lies the head that wears a crown.

  ....*Shakespeare*

- ☐ A price who desires to maintain his position must learn to be not always good, but to be so or not, as needs require.

  ....*Machiavelli*

- ☐ A leader is a dealer in hope.

  ....*Napoleon*

- ☐ An army, leaderless, is slain.

  ....*Panchathantra*

- ☐ I am the State.

  ....*Louis XIV*

- ☐ Princes are like to heavenly bodies, which cause good or evil times, and which have much veneration but no rest.

  ....*Bacon*

- ☐ Nobility has its obligations.

  ....*Due De Levis*

- ☐ I had rather be right than be president.

  ....*Henry Clay*

LEARNING

- ☐ A little learning is a dangerous thing; Drink deep, or taste not pierian spring.

.........*Pope*

- ☐ If you throw a handle of jewels into the head of a child, no one will take it away from him.

.........*A Hindi Proverb*

- ☐ Training is everything. The peach was once a bitter almond; cauliflower is nothing but a cabbage with a college education.

.........*Mark Twain*

- ☐ If by being overstudious, we impair our health and spoil our good humor, let us give it up.

.........*Montaigue*

- ☐ Education.... has produced a vast population able to read but unable to distingish what is worth reading.

.........*G.M. Trevelyan*

- ☐ I find that the three major administrative problems on a campus are sex for the students, athletics for the alumni, and parking for the faculty.

.........*Clark Kerr*

LEISURE

- ☐ A poor life this if, full of care, we have no time to stand and stare.

  ........*W.H. Davies*

- ☐ Leisure with dignity.

  ....*Cicero*

- ☐ Kiddies and grown ups too-oo-oo
  If we haven't enough to do-oo-oo
  we get the hump,cameelious hump,
  The hump that is black and blue.

  ....*Kipling*

- ☐ God loves an idle rainbow, no less than labouring seas.

  ....*Ralph Hodgson*

- ☐ Heap on more wood! the wind is still,
  But let is whistle as it will,
  Well keep our christmas merry still.

  ....*Sir Walter Scott*

- ☐ "Bah", Said Scrooge,"Humbug"!

  ....*Charles Dickens*

- ☐ A cold coming we had of it, Just the worst time of the year.

  ........*T.S. Eliot*

LIBERTY

- ☐ What in some is called liberty, in others is called licence.

  ....*Quintilian*

- ☐ When liberty is gone, Life grows insipid and has lost its relish.

  ....*Addison*

- ☐ What light is to the eyes-what air is to the lungs-what love is to the heart, liberty is to the soul of man.

  ........*R.G. Ingersoll*

- ☐ Liberty, when it begins to take root, is a plant of rapid growth.

  ....*George Washington*

- ☐ Eternal spirit of the chainless Mind! Brightest in dungeons,
  Libèrty! thou art, For there thy habitation is the heart—
  The heart which love of thee alone can bind.

  ....*Byron*

- ☐ "Make way for liberty!" He cried, Made way for liberty, and died.

  ....*James Montgomery*

- ☐ Eternal Vigilance is the price of liberty.

  ....*Wendell Phillips*

LIFE

- ☐ A useless life is an early death.

  ....*Goethe*

- ☐ Birth, copulation, and death, That's all the facts when you come to brass tacks.

  ........*T.S. Eliot*

- ☐ Life is a jest; and all things show it. I thought so once; but now I know it.

  ....*John Gay*

- ☐ Oh, the wild Joys of living!.

  ....*Robert Browning.*

- ☐ And here we are as on a darkling plain swept with confused alarms of struggle and flight, where ignorant armies clash by night.

  ....*Matthew Arnold*

- ☐ We are involved in a life that passes understanding and our highest business is our daily life.

  ....*John Cage*

- ☐ All the world's a Stage, And all the men and women merely players.

  ....*Shakespeare*

- ☐ Life is one long struggle in the dark.

  ....*Lucretius*

LOVE

- ☐ Love is a familiar. Love is a devil. There is no evil angel but love.

  ....*Shakespeare*

- ☐ It is love, not reason, that is stronger than death.

  ....*Christopher Marlowe*

- ☐ We are easily duped by those we love.

  ....*Moliere*

- ☐ Love blinds all men alike, both the reasonable and the foolish.

  ....*Menander*

- ☐ By the time you swear you're his, shivering and sighing,
  And he vows his passion is Infinite, undying-
  Lady make a note of this.
  One of you is lying.

  ....*Dorothy Parker*

- ☐ In their first passion, women love their lovers; in all the others, they love love.

  ....*Ibid*

- ☐ For heaven be thanked, we live in such an age,
  When no man dies for love, but on the stage.

  ....*John Dryden*

LUST

- ☐ The conquest of lust is the highest endeavour of a man's or woman's existence, without overcoming lust man cannot hope to rule over self.

  ........*M.K. Gandhi*

- ☐ After coition every animal is sad.

  ....*Latin Proverb*

- ☐ Men make love more intensely at twenty,
  but make love better, However, at thirty.

  ....*Catherine The Great*

- ☐ Sex is Never an Emergency.

  ....*Dr. Elaine Pierson*

- ☐ Sex and beauty are inseparable, like life and consciousness.

  ........*D.H. Lawrence*

- ☐ There are worse occupations in this world than feeling a woman's pulse.

  ....*Laurence Sterne*

- ☐ I find I care less and less, who goes to bed with whom.

  ....*Dorothy Sayers*

- ☐ Sexuality is the lyricism of the masses.

  ....*Charles Bandelaire*

MAN

- ☐ Men are but children of a larger growth.

  ....*Dryden*

- ☐ Man is a reed, the weakest in nature, but he is a thinking reed.

  ....*Pascal*

- ☐ And much it grieved my heart to think what man has made of man.

  ....*Wordsworth*

- ☐ Man, biologically considered... is the most formidable of all the beasts of prey, and, indeed, the only one that preys systematically on its own species.

  ....*William James*

- ☐ Know than thy self,
  presume not of God to scan, The proper study of mankind is man.

  ....*Pope*

- ☐ Man's inhumanity to man, makes countless thousands mourn.

  ....*Burns*

- ☐ How poor, how rich, how object, how august, How complicate,
  how wonderful is man.

  ....*Young*

- ☐ It is not the greatness of a man's means that make him independent,
  So much as the smallness of his wants.

  ....*Cobbett*

MANNERS

- ☐ An injury is much sooner forgotten than an insult.

  ....*Earl of Chesterfield*

- ☐ Take the tone of the company you are in.

  ....*Ibid*

- ☐ Behave to everyone as if you were receiving a great guest;..... (do not) do to others what you would not wish done to yourself.

  ....*Confucius*

- ☐ Good breeding consists in concealing how much we think of ourselves and how little we think of the other person.

  ....*Mark Twain*

- ☐ You never want to give a man a present when he's feeling good. You want to do it when he's down.

  ....*Lyndon. B.Johnson*

- ☐ Is there no respect of place, persons, nor time, in you?

  ....*Shakespeare*

- ☐ Tact consists in knowing how far we may go too far.

  ....*Jean Coctean*

MARRIAGE

- ☐ A young married is a man that's marred.

  ....*Shakespeare*

- ☐ Advice to those about to marry-Don't.

  ....*Henry Mayhew*

- ☐ Where there's marriage without love, there will be love without marriage.

  ....*Franklin*

- ☐ A good marriage would be between a blind wife and a deaf husband.

  ....*Montaigue*

- ☐ As the husband is, the wife is thou art mated with a clown.
  And the grossness of his nature will have weight drag thee down.

  ....*Tennyson*

- ☐ For the race is run by one and one and never by two and two.

  ....*Kipling*

- ☐ Some pray to marry the man they love, my prayer will somewhat vary;
  I humble pray to Heaven above, that of I love thee man I marry.

  ....*Rose Pastor Stokes*

MEMORY

- ☐ Better by far you should forget and smile,
  Than that you should remember and be sad.

  ....*Christina Rossetti*

- ☐ There is no greater sorrow than to recall, in misery,
  the time when we were happy.

  ....*Dante*

- ☐ I remember, I remember, The house where I was born,
  The little window where the sun, Came peeping in at morn.

  ....*Thomas Hood*

- ☐ Hope links her to the future,-but the link that binds her to the past is memory.

  ....*Amelia B. Welby*

- ☐ Good memories are lost jewels.

  ....*Paul Valery*

- ☐ Memory is the mother of all wisdom.

  ....*Aeschylus*

- ☐ Memory is the treasury and guardian of all things.

  ....*Cicero*

- ☐ Some memories are realities, and are better than anything that can ever happen to one again.

  ....*Willa Cather*

MIND

- ☐ Imagination is more important than knowledge.

  ....*Albert Einstein*

- ☐ There is nothing either good or bad but thinking makes it so.

  ....*Shakespeare*

- ☐ Reason is God's crowning gift to man.

  ....*Sophocles*

- ☐ Meditation is not a means to an end. It is both the means and the end.

  ....*Krishnamurti*

- ☐ A sound mind in a sound body.

  ....*Juvenal*

- ☐ What is mind? No matter. what is matter? Never mind.

  ........*T.H. Key*

- ☐ The lightning-bug is brilliant, but he hasn't any mind.
  He stumbles through existance with his head-light on behind.

  ........*E.F. Ware*

- ☐ God is mind and God is infinite, hence all is mind.

  ....*Mary Baker Eddy*

MISFORTUNE

- ☐ When sorrows come, they come not single spices, But in battalions.

  ....*Shakespeare*

- ☐ If fortune turns against you, even jelly breaks your tooth.

  ....*Persian Proverb*

- ☐ In the misfortunes of our best friends, we find something that is not unpleasing.

  ....*La Rochefoucauld*

- ☐ Into each life some rain must fall, Some days must be dark and dreary

  ....*Henry Wadsworth Longfellow*

- ☐ I never knew any man in my life who could not bear another's misfortunes perfectly like a christian.

  ....*Alexander Pope*

- ☐ Fire is the test of gold, adversity of strong men.

  ....*Seneca*

- ☐ The worst is yet to come.

  ....*Tennyson*

- ☐ Grief teaches the steadiest minds to waver.

  ....*Sophocles*

MONEY

☐ It is very difficult for the prosperous to be humble.

........*Jane Austen*

☐ Money you know will hide many faults.

........*Cervantes*

☐ Money's the wise man's religion.

........*Euripides*

☐ Money is like an arm or leg : use it or lose it.

........*Henry Ford.*

☐ THe universal regard for money is the one hopeful fact in our civilization.

........*Bernard Shaw*

☐ A full pocketbook often groans more loudly than an empty stomach.

........*Roosevelt*

☐ Money is honey, my little sonny, and a rich man's joke is always funny.

........*T.E. Brown*

☐ Never ask of money spent, where the spender thinks it went.
Nobody was ever meant to remember or invent
what he did with every cent.

........*Robert Frost*

NONSENSE *(Famous verses)*

- If the man who turnips cries, cry not when his father dies,
  'Tis proof that he had rather, have a turnip than a father.

  ....*Samuel Johnson*

- One, whom we see not, is, and one, who is not, we see,
  Fiddle, we know, is diddle; and diddle, we take it, is dee

  ....*Swinburne*

- He thought he saw an elephant, that practised on a fife,
  He looked again, and found it was, A letter from his wife.
  "At length I realise", he said, "the bitterness of Life!"

  ....*Lewis carroll*

- The pobble who has no toes, Had once as many as we,
  When they said," Some day you may lose them all",
  He replied, 'Fish fiddle-de-dee!" and his Aunt Jobiska make him drink,
  Lavender water tinged with pink, for she said, "The world in general knows
  There's nothing so good for a pebble's toes!"

  ....*Eduward Lear*

OPINION

- ☐ Opinion's but a fool, that makes us scan the outward habit by the inward man.

  ....*Shakespeare*

- ☐ He that complies against his will, Is of his own opinion still,
  Which he may adhere to, yet disown, for reasons to himself best known.

  ....*Butler*

- ☐ Some praise at morning what they blame at night,
  But always think the last opinion right.

  ....*Pope*

- ☐ Public opinion, a vulgar, impertinent, anonymous tyrant who deliberately makes life unpleasant for anyone who is not content to be the average man.

  ....*Dean W.R. Inge*

- ☐ The man who never alters his opinion is like standing water,
  and breeds reptiles of the mind.

  ....*Black*

- ☐ The pressure of public opinion is like the pressure of the atmosphere, you can't see it-but, all the same, it is sixteen pounds to the square inch.

  ........*J.R.Lowell*

OPPORTUNITY

- There is a tide in the affairs of men,
which taken at the flood, leads on to fortune.

........Shakespeare

- With doubt and dismay you are smitten,
You think there's no chance for you, son?
Why the best books haven't been written,
The best race has't been run.

........Berton Braley

- They do me wrong who say I come no more when once I knock and fail to find you in, for every day I stand outside your door and bid you wake, and rise to fight and win.

........Walter Malone

- O, once in each man's life, at least, good luck knocks at his door,
And with no seize the witting Guest, need never hunger more.

........L.J.Bates

- Make hay while the sun shines.

........A. Proverb

- Master of human destinies am I!, Fame, love, and fortune on my footsteps wait, Cities and fields I walk, I penetrate, Deserts and seas remote, and passing by, Hovel and mart and palace, soon or late, I knock unbidden once at every gate...

........J.J. Ingallis

OPTIMISM

- ☐ All is for the best in the best of possible worlds.

  ....*Voltaire*

- ☐ A health unto the happy, a fig for him who frets!
  It is not raining rain to me, It's raining violets

  ....*R.Loveman*

- ☐ Cheer up, the worst is yet to come.

  ....*Philander Johnson*

- ☐ The optimist proclaims that we live in the best of all possible worlds,
  and the pessimist fears this is true.

  ....*James Branch Cabell*

- ☐ Behold, we know not anything, I can but trust that good shall fall
  At last-for off-at last, to all, All every winter change to spring.

  ....*Tennyson*

- ☐ One who never turned his back but marched breast forward.
  Never doubted clouds would break,
  Never dreamed, tough right were worsted, wrong would triumph,
  Held we fall to rise, are baffled to fight better, sleep to wake.

  ....*R.Browning*

PARENTS

- Children begin by loving their parents;
  as they grow older they judge them; sometimes they forgive them.

  ....*Oscar Wilde*
- Honour they father and thy mother; that thy days may be long upon the land which the Lord thy God giveth thee.

  ....*Old Testament*
- Of all the animals, the boy is the most unmanageable.

  ....*Plato*
- The child is father of the man.

  ....*William Wordsworth*
- A child should always say what's true, And speak when he is spoken to.
  And behave mannerly at table; at least as far as he is able.

  ....*Robert Louis Stevenson*
- Between the dark and the daylight, when the night is beginning to lower
  Comes a pause in the day's occupations, that is known as the children hour.

  ....*Henry Wordsworth Longfellow*
- A little child shall lead them.

  ....*Bible*

PARTING

- ☐ Excuse me, then! you know my heart,
  But dearest friends, alas! must part.

  ....*John Gay*

- ☐ To meet, to know, the love-and then to part,
  Is the sad tale of many a human heart.

  ........*S.T.Coleridge*

- ☐ Good night, good night! parting is such sweet sorrow,
  That I shall say good night till it be morrow.

  ....*Shakespeare*

- ☐ When we two parted, In silence and tears, Half broken-hearted,
  To sever for years, Pale grew thy cheek and cold, Colder thy Kiss....

  ....*Byron*

- ☐ Some weep because they part,and languish broken hearted,
  And others-O my heart!, Because they never parted.

  ........*T.B. Aldrich*

- ☐ Since there's no help, come, let us kiss and part;
  Nay, I have done, you get no more of me; And I am glad, yea,
  Glad with all my heart,
  That thus go cleanly I myself can free.

  ....*Michael Drayton*

PATIENCE

- ☐ Since you will buckle fortune on my back,
  To bear her burthen, whether I will or no,
  I must have patience to endure the load.

  ....*Shakespeare*
- ☐ Patience is the virtue of an ass, That trots beneath his burthen, and is quiet.

  ....*George Granville*
- ☐ They also serve who only stand and wait.

  ....*John Milton*
- ☐ Patience is the companion of wisdom.

  ....*St. Augustine*
- ☐ Patience and delay achieve more than force and rage.

  ....*La Fontaine*
- ☐ Every thing comes if a man will only wait.

  ....*Benjamin Disraeli*
- ☐ Patience conquers everything.

  ....*Dutch Proverb*
- ☐ How far then, catiline, will you abuse our patience?

  ....*Cicero*
- ☐ Beware the fury of a patient man.

  ....*Dryden*

PERSONALITY

- ☐ Personality is to man what perfume is to a flower.

  ....*Charles M.Schwab*

- ☐ I am the owner of the sphere, of the seven stars and the solar year, of Caesar's hand, and Plato's brain, of Lord Christ's heart, and Shakespeare's strain.

  ....*Emerson*

- ☐ There are three Johns; I, the real John; known only to his maker; Z, John's ideal John, never the real one, and often very unlike him; 3, Thomas's ideal John, never the real John, nor John's John, but often very unlike either.

  ....*O. W. Holmes*

- ☐ Fame is what you have taken, character's what you give, when to this truth you waken, then you begin to live.

  ....*Bayard Taylor*

- ☐ Don't say things, what you are stands over you the while, and thunders so that I cannot hear what you say to the contrary.

  ....*Emerson*

PLEASURE

- In play, there are two pleasures for your choosing.
  The one is winning, and the other losing.

  ....*Byron*

- But pleasures are like poppies spread,you seize the flow'r its bloom is shed!
  Or like the snow-fall in a river, a moment while-then melts for ever.

  ....*Burns*

- Rich the treasure, Sweet the pleasure, Sweet is pleasure after pain.

  ....*Dryden*

- All human race from China to Peru,
  Pleasure, however disguis'd by art, pursue.

  ....*T.Warton*

- I seek the atmost pleasure and the least pain.

  ....*Plautus*

- Gather ye rosebuds while ye may; old time is still a-flying,
  and this same flower that smiles today, tomorrow will be dying.

  ....*Robert Herrick*

- Do what you will .

  ....*Rabelais*

PRAYER

☐ Prayer is the little implement, Through which men reach
Where presence-is denied them.

.........*Emily D:ckinson*

☐ Ask the Gods nothing excessive.

.........*Aeschylus*

☐ Pray, for all men need the aid of the Gods.

.........*Homer*

☐ You pray in your distress and in you r need; would that you might pray also in the fullness of your joy and in your days of abundance.

.........*Kahlil Gibran*

☐ I am groping for the keys, of the heavily harmonies.

.........*Whittier*

☐ If by prayer, Incessant I could hope to change the will
Of him who all things can, I would not cease
To weary him with my assiduous cries.

.........*Milton*

☐ In prayer the lips nev'er act the winning part without the sweet concurrence of the heart.

.........*Herrick*

QUARREL

- Those who in quarrels interpose, must often wipe a bloody nose.

........Gay

- Beware of entrance to a quarrel; but being in,
Bear't that the opposed may beware of thee.

........Shakespeare

- The test of mans or a woman's breeding is how he or she behaves in a quarrel.

........A Hindi Proverb

- In quarreling the truth is lost.

........Syrian Proverb

- .... We quarrel in print, by the book ...., The first, the retort courteous; the second, the quip modest; the third, the reply churlish, the fourth, the reproof valiant, the fifth, the counter check quarrelsome, the sixth, the Lie with circumstance, the seventh, the lie Direct; all these you may avoid but the lie direct; and you may avoid that too, with an if...

........Shakespeare

- It takes two to quarrel, (you cannot clap with one hand).

........A Hindi Proverb

READING

- Who readeth much, and never meditates, Is like the greedy eaten of much food, what so surcloys his stomach with his cates,
  That commonly they do him little good.

  ....*Joshua Sylvester*

- Reading maketh a full man, conference a ready man,
  and writing an exact man.

  ....*Bacon*

- The three practical rules, then, which I have to offer, are,-
  1. Never read any book that is not a year old.
  2. Never read any but the famed books.
  3. Never read any but what you like.

  ....*Emerson*

- Verily, when the day of Judgment comes,
  We shall not be asked what we have read, but what we have done.

  ....*Thomas, A.Kempis*

- I love to lose myself in other men's minds; when I am not walking,
  I am reading, I cannot sit and think. Books think for me.

  ....*Charles Lamb*

- A man may as well expect to grow stronger by always eating as wiser by always reading.

  ....*Jeremy collier*

RELIGION

- Science without religion is lame, religion without science is blind.

  ....*Albert Einstein*

- All religions are ancient monuments to superstitions, ignorance, ferocity; and modern religions are only ancient follies rejuvenated.

  ....*Baron D. Holbach*

- I want nothing to do with any religion concerned with keeping the masses satisfied to live in hunger, filth, and ignorance.

  ....*Jawaharlal Nehru*

- I never saw, heard, nor read that the clergy were beloved in any nation where christianity was the religion of the country. Nothing can render them popular but some degree of persecution.

  ....*Jonathan Swift*

- Religion....is the opium of the people.

  ....*Karl Marx*

- All religions must be tolerated....for..... every man must get to heaven his own way.

  ....*Frederick The Great*

- One religion is as another.

  ....*Hindi Proverb*

REVENGE

- ☐ Revenge is a kind of wild justice, which the more man's nature runs to the more ought law to weed it out.

  ....*Francis Bacon*

- ☐ Revenge is the poor delight of little minds.

  ....*Juvenal*

- ☐ Men regard it as their right to return evil for evil-and if they cannot, feel they have lost their liberty.

  ....*Aristotle*

- ☐ A man that studieth revenge keeps his own wounds green, which otherwise would heal and do well.

  ....*Ibid*

- ☐ If a Jew wrong a Christian, what is his humility? Revenge. If a christian wrong a Jew, what should his suffrance be by christain example? Why revenge. The villainy you teach me, I will execute, and it shall go hard but I will better the instruction.

  ....*Shakespeare*

- ☐ Living well is the best revenge.

  ....*George Herbert*

SIMPLICITY

- In the complicated agitation of modern existance, our wearied souls dream of simplicity.

  ....*Charls Wagner*

- Manifest Plainness, Embrace Simplicity, Reduce Selfishness, Have few desires.

  ....*Lao-tzu*

- Less is more.

  ....*Robert Browning*

- SImplify, Simplify.

  ....*Thorean*

- Beauty of style and harmony and grace and good rhythm depend on Simplicity.

  ....*Plato*

- Teach us delight in simple things ,and mirth that has no bitter springs.

  ....*Rudyard Kipling*

- Except ye be converted and become as little children, ye shall not enter into the kingdom of heaven.

  ....*Ibid*

SIN

- ☐ There is nothing in the world like the devotion of a married woman. It's a thing no married man knows anything about.

  ....*Oscar Wilde*

- ☐ Pleasure's a Sin, and sometimes sin's a pleasure.

  ....*Ibid*

- ☐ Really to sin you have to be serious about it.

  ....*Henrik Ibsen*

- ☐ What men call gallantry, and Gods adultery,
  Is much more common where the climate's sultry.

  ....*Lord Byron*

- ☐ The probable fact is that we are descended not only from monkeys but from monks.

  ....*Elbert Hybbard*

- ☐ Owning her weakness, Her evil behavior,
  And leaving with meekness,Her sings to her saviour!

  ....*Thomas Hood*

- ☐ I am a man, more sinn'd against than sinning.

  ....*Shakespeare*

- ☐ The wages of sin is death.

  ....*New Testament.*

SORROW

- To sorrow I bade good sorrow;
  And thought to leave her far away behind;
  But cheerly, cheerly , she loves me dearly;
  She is no constant to me, and so kind.

  ....*Keats*

- Earth has so sorrow that heaven cannot heal.

  ....*Thomas Moore*

- Heavy the sorrow that bows the head when love is alive and hope is dead.

  ........*W.S. Gilbert*

- The deeper the sorrow, the less tongue hath it.

  ....*Jewish Proverb*

- Weeping may endure for a night, but joy cometh in the morning.

  ....*Bible*

- Pure and complete sorrow is as impossible as pure and complete joy.

  ....*Leo Tolstoy*

- The cares that infest the day, Shall fold their tents, like the Arabs,
  And as silently steal away.

  ....*Henry Wadsworth Longfellow*

THINKING

- ☐ Our life is what our thoughts make it.

  ....*Marcus Aurelins*

- ☐ The mind is its own place, and in itself
  can make a heaven of Hell, a hell of Heaven.

  ....*John Milton*

- ☐ Being and thought are one.

  ....*Jean Dubuffet*

- ☐ On earth there is nothing great but man,
  in man there is nothing great but mind.

  ....*Sir William Hamilton*

- ☐ There is nothing neither good or bad, thinking makes it so.

  ....*Shakespeare*

- ☐ They are never alone that are accompanied with noble thoughts.

  ....*Sir. Philip Sidney*

- ☐ What we call a mind is nothing but a heap or collection of different perceptions, united together by certain relations, and supposed, though falsely, to be endowed with a perfect simplicity and identity.,

  ....*David Hume*

- ☐ A good mind is a lord of a kingdom.

  ....*Seneca*

TRUTH

- Truth is tough.

  ....*Oliver Wendell Holmes*

- Truth even lovely-since the world began,
  The foe of tyrants and the friends of man.

  ....*Thomas Campbell*

- The exact opposite of what is generally, believed is often the truth.

  ....*La Bruyere*

- Rather than love, than money, than fame, give me truth.

  ....*Thorean*

- Truth is no road to fortune.

  ....*Jean Jacques Rousseau*

- The love of truth has its reward in heaven and even on earth.

  ....*Friedrich Neitzsche*

- A truth that's told with a bad intent, Beats all the lies you can invent.

  ....*Blake*

- How happy is he born and taught, That serveth not another's will;
  Whose armour is his honest thought, And simple truth his utmost skill.

  ....*Sir Henry Watton*

UNITED

- ☐ United we stand, divided we fall.

  ....Aesop

- ☐ Who end bad men combine, the good must associate, else they will fall, one by one, an unpitied sacrifice in a contemptible struggle.

  ....Edmund Burke

- ☐ There are only two forces that unite men-fear and interest.

  ....Napoleon Bonaparte

- ☐ One flag, one land, one heart, one hand, one nation, evermore!.

  ........O.W.Holmes

- ☐ All your strength is in your union, all your danger is in discord.

  ....Longfellow

- ☐ One from many.

  ....Virgil

- ☐ Something there is that doesn't love a wall.

  ....Robert Frost

- ☐ If a house be divided against itself, that house cannot stand.

  ....Bible

WEALTH

- ☐ The rich would have to eat money, but luckily the poor provide food.

  ....*Russian Proverb*
- ☐ If you are poor today, you will always be poor, only the rich acquire riches.

  ....*Martial*
- ☐ Half the world does not know how the other half lives.

  ....*Rabelais*
- ☐ Superfluous wealth can buy superfluities only. Money is not required to buy one necessary of the Soul.

  ....*Thoreay*
- ☐ Ill fares the land, to hastening ills a prey, where wealth accumulates, and men decay.

  ....*Gold smith*
- ☐ The poor is hated even of his own, neighbour, but the rich have many friends.

  ....*Bible*
- ☐ Really, if the lower orders don't set us a good example, what on earth is the use of them.

  ....*Oscar Wilde*

WOMAN

- ☐ Alas! the love of women! it is known to be a lovely and a fearful thing.

  ....*Lord Byron*

- ☐ Most women have no characters at all.

  ....*Alexander Pope*

- ☐ The female of the species is more deadly than the male.

  ....*Rudyard Kipling*

- ☐ There is nothing worse than a woman, Even a good woman.!

  ....*Menander*

- ☐ The woman is so hard, upon the woman.

  ....*Alfred, Lord Tennyson*

- ☐ There's no fury like a woman searching for a new lover.

  ....*Cyril Connolly*

- ☐ Woman was God's second mistake.

  ....*Friedrich Nietzsche*

- ☐ Woman fail to understand how much men hate them.

  ....*Germaine Greer*

WRITING

- There's nothing to writting,
  All you do is sit down at a typewriter and open a vein.

  ....*Walter Red Smith*

- All writing comes by the grace of God.

  ....*Emerson*

- Being a great writer is not the same as writing great.

  ....*John Updike*

- You write with ease to show your breeding,
  But easy writing's curst hard reading.

  ........*R.B.Sheridan*

- Let him be kept from paper, pen, and ink,
  So may he cease to write and learn to think.

  ....*Prior*

- Such was the muse whose rules and practice tell,
  'Nature's chief masterpiece is writing well."

  ....*Pope*

- .....Biting my truant pen, beating myself for spite;
  Fool! said my muse to me, look in thy heart and write.

  ....*Sir Philip Sidney*

YOUTH

- O youth with song and laugher, Go not so lightly by;
  Have pity-and remember, How soon thy roses die.

  ....*A. W. Peach*

- "And youth is cruel, and has no remorse and smiles at situations which it cannot see." I smile, of course, and go on drinking tea.

  ........*T.S. Eliot*

- Then come kiss me, sweet-and-twenty, youth's a stuff will not endure.

  ....*Shakespeare*

- In youth the heart exults and sings, the pulses leap, the feet have wings;
  In age the cricket chirps, and brings the harvest home of days.

  ....*Longfellow*

- Bliss was it in that dawn to be alive, But to be young was very heaven!

  ....*Wordsworth*

- Youth is the pollen, That blows through the sky; And does not ask why.

  ....*Stephen Vincent Benet*